Lost
Childhood

My Life in a Japanese Prison
Camp During World War II

A Memoir by
ANNELEX HOFSTRA LAYSON

WITH HERMAN J. VIOLA

NATIONAL
GEOGRAPHIC
WASHINGTON, D.C.

To my grandmother, whom I called Oma, my mother, and my brother, Jack.
I would not be here but for the constancy of their love and attentive care.

Acknowledgments

Not even in my wildest dreams did I ever think this story would be told. Many, many thanks to my co-author, Herman Viola, for his literary skills and for giving me the courage to write about my experiences in Japanese concentration camps. To Sarah Shoob, whose warmth and understanding helped me to clarify my thoughts on paper. Thanks for drying my tears when very unpleasant memories were difficult to talk about. To Suzanne Fonda, our editor, whose kind words and wisdom are priceless. Thank you, Suzanne, for your guidance and friendship. To my wonderful children, Ingrid and Neil, whose idea it was to write this book. To my daughter-in-law, AmyBeth, for your enthusiasm and patience when Neil was helping with the beginnings of the manuscript. To grandsons Kyle, Evan, and Landon, for whom this book was written, with love more than they will ever know. To other family members and many friends too numerous to mention, whose encouragement was so helpful in obtaining my goal to write this book. But most important, I'd like to thank my wonderful husband, Bill. Without his gentle prodding and advice, this book would never have been written.

For information about special discounts for bulk purchases, please contact
National Geographic Books Special Sales: ngspecsales@ngs.org.

For rights or permissions inquiries, please contact National Geographic Books Subsidiary Rights:
ngbookrights@ngs.org.

Cover design by Marty Ittner.
Book design by David M. Seager.
The body text is set in Mrs. Eaves. The display text is Bureau Agency.

Library of Congress Cataloging-in-Publication Data
Layson, Annelex Hofstra.
Lost childhood : my life in a Japanese prison camp during World War II / Annelex Hofstra Layson ; with Herman Viola.
p. cm.
ISBN 978-1-4263-0321-0 (hbk. : alk. paper)
ISBN 978-1-4263-0322-7 (lib. bndg. : alk. paper)
1. Layson, Annelex Hofstra—Childhood and youth. 2. World War, 1939-1945—Prisoners and prisons, Japanese. 3. World War, 1939-1945—Children—Indonesia—Biography. 4. World War, 1939-1945—Personal narratives, Dutch. 5. Concentration camp inmates—Indonesia—Biography. 6. Child concentration camp inmates—Indonesia—Biography. I. Viola, Herman J. II. Title.
D805.J3L34 2008
940.53'175982092—dc22
[B]
                    2008011671

Front cover: Four-year-old Annelex clutches her doll, Greta, her constant companion in the Japanese prison camps.

Printed in the United States of America

Contents

Foreword 7

◇◇

◇◇

Foreword

HERMAN J. VIOLA

LOST CHILDHOOD IS A VIVID, FIRSTHAND ACCOUNT OF A LITTLE GIRL who spent three-and-a-half years of her life with her mother and grandmother in Japanese prison camps in the Dutch East Indies (now Indonesia) during World War II.

For 60 years Annelex (or Lex as she prefers to be called) never talked about her imprisonment, not even with her first husband of 33 years or their children. The memories were too painful. What made her start talking? It all started when I met Lex at a reception in honor of Joseph Lekuton, the author of *Facing the Lion,* the first book in the memoir series in which *Lost Childhood* now appears.

As an ethnologist and an archivist at the Smithsonian Institution, I have always had an interest in collecting stories about the human experience. When Lex's husband, Bill Layson, confided to me that his wife had a story as remarkable and courageous as Joseph's, I was curious to learn more.

At first Lex did not want to write a book, saying no one would be interested in her story. I assured her otherwise and pointed out that those who have the ability and opportunity to do so should document this tragic episode in world history for future generations to learn and hopefully benefit from. Reluctantly and sometimes tearfully, she began to reveal her past.

In telling her story, Lex wants to honor all those Dutch men, women, and children who suffered or died in the Japanese camps. She realizes that soon all the survivors will be gone. If their stories are not collected and recorded now, they will be lost forever. She also wants to share a lesson she learned from her experience.

She believes that the reason her family not only survived the camps but also have gone on to lead long, productive lives is that her mother never gave in to despair. She was driven by the goal of making sure her family survived to live a better life. She never gave up, even in the face of devastating losses. Lex has inherited this same strong spirit and credits it with helping her realize the need to focus on the positive rather than allowing negative experiences and thoughts to rule her life. Such a path takes constant work, but the rewards—sometimes long in coming—are worth the effort and the wait.

Lost Childhood is a memoir, not a diary. Some details have blurred over time, and some memories are more vivid than others. But the core of her story is fact, and it is reproduced as faithfully as possible. My special thanks to Sara Shoob, who helped record some of the more personal parts of Lex's story.

Even as a four-year-old I could tell something bad was happening.

Before

BEFORE WORLD WAR II BROKE OUT IN THE PACIFIC, MY FAMILY led a very comfortable life. We lived in a large stucco house in a Dutch neighborhood in the town of Surabaya, near the eastern end of the island of Java in what is now Indonesia. As was typical of many other European families on the island, we had servants—a cook (Kokkie), a maid (Baboe), and a butler (Djongos), who also fixed things when they broke, painted, and did other odd jobs around the house. We were Dutch, but our servants were Javanese, people whose families had been on the island for thousands of years. They lived in our house, and to me they were part of the family. I never thought about what it meant for them that Europeans had taken over their country.

Back then Indonesia was the Dutch East Indies. For 340 years it had been a colony of the Netherlands. We spoke Dutch and thought of the Netherlands as "back home," even though all of us except my father had been born in the East Indies. But we loved our beautiful island, a tropical paradise of white sand beaches, rugged mountains, and lush green forests. In the summer when the bustling port city of Surabaya was at its most uncomfortably hot, we went to our summer house in the mountains near Nonkojajar in East Java. There, we loved to watch monkeys play under the waterfalls next to our house.

Our household was made up of my father,

my mother, my brother, and my grandmother, who came to live with us after the death of my grandfather. I don't remember him because he died before my first birthday. But I do know that it is thanks to him that I am called Annelex. "Anne" was my grandmother's name; "lex" was short for Alexander—his name.

Oma is the Dutch word for "grandmother." We sometimes called her *Omaatje,* meaning "little grandmother," because she was short. Because I was the youngest in the family, I was called *Annelexje,* "little Annelex."

I adored my grandmother. My mother did a lot of volunteer work at the hospital, and my brother, Jack, went to school, so Oma and I had plenty of time to spend together. We went shopping almost everyday. In town she would flag down a kind of taxi called a *betjak,* a cart with two seats that was powered from the rear by a man pedalling a bicycle. Then we would go exploring among the street vendors. She would buy me little rings and other sparkly trinkets. Often before heading home we would stop for ice cream. It was heavenly.

My memories of that time before the war come to me in snippets, like snapshots or tiny movies. We had a big front porch, which we called the veranda. If I close my eyes now, I can see my family and our neighbors sitting outside at twilight, the grown-ups chatting, ensconced in cushioned rattan chairs; the children gathered on the steps or playing hide-and-seek. The house had been a wedding gift from my mother's parents. Most of our neighbors were either relatives or families whose fathers—like mine— were in the military. Surabaya was home to the largest naval base in the Dutch East Indies.

The best part of each evening—at least for us children—was a visit from a Chinese peddler pushing a cart laden with goodies for sale. My parents loved Chinese food, and they would buy fried dumplings and egg rolls for everyone—just a little, "a taste," my mother called it. When Djongos announced that it was time for dinner, the guests drifted off to the comforts of their own homes while we went in to enjoy ours.

Kokkie made all different kinds of food for us—Indonesian and Chinese as well as Dutch. All of our meat (chicken and pork) and fish came from local sources. Because we had a year-round growing season, there were always fresh fruits and vegetables—mangoes, papayas, bananas, carrots, peppers, and Chinese lettuce, which was something like coleslaw. We had chocolate milk, fruit-flavored candy, sugar, and tea. My favorite lunch was a peanut-butter-and-jelly sandwich, and Kokkie always had something yummy in the kitchen for snacks.

My brother, Jack, was my hero. He gave me

rides on the back of his bicycle, which was outfitted with a cushion and much faster than my scooter. At ten, Jack was twice my size, strong enough to put me on his back and gallop around the yard. Of course he loved to tease me, but I was always ready to do anything for him.

We had a great big mango tree in our front yard. It was wonderful for climbing. One day my brother and two of our boy cousins came up with a plan for a flying machine and offered me the chance to be the first to try it out. I watched as Jack climbed up to the first big limb, tossed a rope over the branch to a cousin below, then scrambled down. He wrapped me up in an old sheet and tied one end of the rope around my waist and through my legs (that was the seat, he told me). Then the three of them proceeded to pull on the other end of the rope, hand over hand, hoisting me into the air.

At first it was fun, like being on a swing.

But as they jerked me higher and higher, the rope tightened around me. I began to spin and bump into the tree. Feeling queasy and in pain, I yelled, *"Nee, Japie, nee Japie. Pijn, pijn!"* meaning, "No Jack, no Jack. Pain, pain!" I must have sounded as though I were getting killed because my mother came rushing out of the house. She wasn't the least bit happy with the scene that greeted her. She ordered the boys to let me down—gently. Needless to say, that was the end of the flying experiment.

I have much better memories of walking with my family to the swimming pool. My mother would keep an eye on Jack, while my father taught me how to float and how to swim. Pappie (that's what I called him) was a very tall, big man. He would hold me in his arms, and we would bounce in the water, splashing and laughing together. I always felt safe with him.

We had lots of pets in our house and yard.

My brother raised doves and chickens. Looking back, I am sure that some of them ended up on our dinner table, but at the time I was clueless. We also had a huge turtle (Bonzo), a big dog (Blackie), a myna bird (a type of tropical starling that likes to mimic sounds and voices), and three cats. One was a gray-and-white-striped male we called Gray. The other two were beautiful, plushy-furred Angoras: Babka (a male) and Mimkie (a female). When I played dress up, the skirt of one of my mother's dresses would drag behind me like a bridal train. The cats, especially Babka and Mimkie, loved to jump on and hitch rides.

Little by little things began to change. It was like water trickling out of a pump. At first there's hardly any water, and then more comes out, stronger and stronger. That's kind of how the war entered our lives.

The grown-ups were talking about it more and more. Every evening after dinner, my father and mother listened to the radio crackle the news. And every evening, the serious looks on their faces deepened. The war had been going on in Europe since September 1939 when Adolf Hitler, leader of Germany, marched his army into Poland. The following May, Belgium, Luxembourg, and the Netherlands, our home country, fell to him. Meanwhile, things were heating up in the Pacific as Japan, stoked by victories in China and on the mainland of Southeast Asia, started eyeing the East Indies and other island territories. The United States responded to Japan's aggression by cutting off shipments of scrap iron, steel, and oil—resources Japan needed to fuel its war machine and expand its empire in the Pacific. The embargo made Japan more determined than ever to take control of the rich oil reserves in the East Indies.

As tensions rose during the fall of 1941, our government began preparing people in the East Indies for possible war. Not far from our house was a huge tower with a siren on it. Whenever that siren went off, it was a signal for everyone to take cover. These practice drills could happen at any time—when we were eating breakfast, playing with friends, or sleeping in our beds. It was a signal to gather together and take shelter under whatever was handy.

One day I saw workmen building something in our front yard under the mango tree. It turned out to be a bomb shelter. It was made of clay, and looked sort of like the huts in Africa that I had seen in magazines. We were one of the few families in our neighborhood that had a shelter. I found out later that my grandmother had paid for it. I realize now that something that was aboveground and made of clay would not have protected us from a real bomb, but it was away from the house and the huge branches of the mango tree made it hard to see from the air.

The shelter was small, and we had to step down to get inside. There were benches around the walls to sit on, no windows, and just an opening for a door so we could peek out to see what was happening. At first I thought it was a great place to play—like having my own little house. But all that changed after the Japanese surprised the Americans by bombing their naval base at Pearl Harbor, in Hawai'i, in December 1941. This was quickly followed by attacks on Hong Kong, the Philippines, and other bases in the western Pacific. It was only a matter of time before they attacked our island.

I can still remember the terrifying feelings I had every time the siren went off. Although they tried to hide it, my mother and my grandmother were scared too. I could see it in their faces and in the darting way they moved, gathering me up and yelling to Jack and the servants to get to the shelter as fast as possible. Of course there was no way to tell if the signal was for a practice drill or a real attack, so every time we heard it, we moved fast, then huddled together in the shelter.

In the bomb shelter, each of us wore a sort of necklace—a string with beads of hard foam rubber. If we heard airplanes overhead, we were supposed to chew on the rubber. Chewing made our mouths water, so we would swallow a lot. Swallowing would help keep our eardrums from bursting from the pressure of any bombs going off nearby.

My father was a pilot in the Dutch Navy. His base was in Surabaya, so he could come home for dinner almost every night. But soon after the attack on Pearl Harbor, he received orders to leave on a mission. None of us—not even my mother—was told where he was going. I found out later that he went first to New Guinea, another island in the East Indies. From there he was supposed to go to Australia, where the Dutch government was sending a lot of its pilots and planes to keep them from being captured by the Japanese. But he never made it. His plane was shot down over the ocean. No one ever told my mother if he was dead or alive, just that he was missing. She lived with that terrible anxiety for years. She never gave up hope, and she never shared her fears with Jack or me. All we knew was that he was helping our country in the war. In fact, it was not until a few years ago that I learned what had happened!

Looking back, I am fairly certain I know the exact day that my mother found out. It was on one of those afternoons when she would invite some of her girlfriends over. Most of their husbands were off on missions too, so they would get together for moral support. My mother would dress me up in a pretty sundress and tie my hair with a ribbon to match. Kokkie would prepare some special goodies, and the whole house would be filled with yummy smells from the kitchen. This particular gathering had a very peculiar ending that for years was a mystery to me. My mother was playing the piano for her guests when the phone rang. She excused herself and went to answer it. When she came back, she was crying. She mumbled something about bumping her nose, but suddenly her friends were hugging her and saying goodbye. The party was over. She went to her room to lie down. At the time it all seemed very strange, but now it makes perfect sense.

That was just the first of several bizarre events that happened that day. Left by myself, I climbed into one of the big, cushy, gold velvet chairs in the living room. Suddenly the chair moved. All by itself, it started sliding across the tile floor. I gripped the chair arms in panic. The chair bumped, then it moved a little bit, then another bump, and it moved a little bit more. Suddenly, I heard my mother yell that we had to go to the bomb shelter. It was an earthquake, and she was afraid the house would collapse. Of course the shelter could not have protected us from the earthquake, but in our panicked state, it made us feel safe.

Fearing aftershocks, we stayed in the shelter quite a while. It was dark when we thought we heard airplanes. Then we heard what sounded like gunshots. The planes were shooting at the houses in our neighborhood. When we peeked out the door of the shelter, we could see streaks of light, called tracers, coming from the bullets. Then a bomb hit the house next to ours, destroying it and killing everyone inside. The explosion was deafening. Terrified, we clung to each other. The day we had dreaded had arrived. The Japanese were attacking.

On March 9, 1942, the Japanese took control
of Java. Not long after, Japanese officers began
coming to our house. They came in twos; one
who could speak a little Dutch, the other—clearly
in charge—spoke only Japanese. Each time it was
a different officer. My mother would call the
family and servants together and then verify each
person's identity by showing the proper papers.
The man in charge wrote everything down.

To me the officers looked like monsters.
They wore big caps with gold braid trim, and
their uniforms were very dark navy blue.
Their boots, which came up to their knees,
somehow seemed to embody danger. I couldn't
understand what they were saying, but the tone
of their voices was as intimidating as the sharp
staccato noise their boots made on the tile floor.
Everything about them frightened me.

The Japanese officers seemed to like our
house. They came more and more often. After

checking to make sure everyone was accounted for, the translator would ask my mother where my father was. When she told him she didn't know, their eyes would narrow, and they would ask more questions. They would look all over the house, slamming doors, then leave.

One day my grandmother told me we were moving. She said that on moving day we would ride in a big wagon with four wheels, one on each corner, pulled by an ox. I thought she meant that we were just going on a fun trip. She never told me that we would not be coming back. She just told me that we would be together.

When people move, they usually take all their possessions with them, but it was not like that for us. We did not take our beds or any furniture, just the bare essentials. For me, that was Greta, my favorite doll. My mother made sure I also had a couple of dresses, underclothes, a blanket, and a *hansopje*—a one-piece playsuit with ruffles. My mother and grandmother packed a few photo albums and some things Oma had embroidered in addition to clothes and a few personal items. I never knew what Jack put in his bag. Altogether we only had a couple of suitcases plus what we could carry.

In all the commotion I never thought about what was going to happen to my cats or the other animals. Surely Kokkie, Baboe, or Djongos would look out for them as they always did when we went on vacation. I was heartbroken when I learned that my mother had been forced to discharge the servants and turn our beloved pets loose to fend for themselves.

By the time moving day came, the whole thing seemed like a big game to me. When the cart came to take us to the station on Darmo Boulevard in Surabaya, I grabbed Greta and scrambled to the top of the pile. I was so excited. I couldn't wait to get on the train.

Gedangan

╳╳╳╳╳╳╳╳╳╳╳╳╳╳╳╳╳╳╳╳╳╳╳╳╳╳╳╳╳╳╳╳╳╳

THE FUN STOPPED WHEN WE GOT TO THE STATION. THERE WAS mass confusion. Hundreds of people were milling about, and Japanese soldiers were marching around in their high boots, shouting orders in Japanese. Of course no one could understand what they were saying, which added to the confusion and made everyone nervous and anxious. It seemed *everyone* was moving, but none of us were moving because we wanted to.

The Japanese had won the native population over by allowing their leader, a Javanese man named Sukarno, to form a government free from the Dutch but answerable to the Japanese. To keep the European population from interfering with their control, the Japanese created internment camps. There were several hundred of these prison camps across the East Indies and other islands in the Pacific that had come under their control. All told, some 300,000 of us were forced to live in them.

At the train station, we learned through an interpreter working for the Japanese that Jack could not stay with my mother, grandmother, and me. Some camps were for women, and others were for men. Jack was ten years old, and boys that age and older were considered men. I couldn't believe what I was hearing. Already my father was far away. Now I was about to be separated from my other protector. I was devastated.

Putting her arms around Jack and me, my mother hugged us close. Then, while Oma tried to comfort me, she gently held Jack's face in her hands and looked into his eyes. She told him that every night he should look at the star in the East, just as we always had at home. The rest of us would do the same. By looking at the same star, we would feel as though we were together if only for a few moments each day. It would be a way to share our love and prayers for a quick reunion. She just barely had time to give him a kiss before a soldier pulled him away. I remember thinking how brave he looked as he waved goodbye and headed toward the other end of the station where the men's trains were.

Suddenly there was a lot of commotion as the guards started shoving all of us women and children toward our trains. My mother picked me up and grabbed Oma's hand so that we wouldn't get separated in the rush. There was lots of yelling, screaming, and crying going on. I was terrified.

My mother and Oma were lucky to get two of the few remaining seats, so I got to sit on their laps. Everyone who got on after us had to stand or sit on the floor. There was not a spot to spare by the time the train got under way.

The train chugged on for hours. The windows were all open, but the train moved too slowly to create a breeze. (Trains didn't have air conditioning back then—at least not in the Indies.) Being so crowded together made us hotter still. It was just sweltering. It must have been at least 120 degrees. On top of that, women were crying, and kids were screaming.

It's funny what sticks in your mind over the years. I remember my mother and my grandmother quietly talking to each other. I remember a scowling Japanese guard pushing his way along the aisle, shouting orders. I remember a puzzled, frightened, out-of-control kind of feeling. I had no idea where we were going, what we were going to do, or what the Japanese were going to do to us. For that whole long train ride, we were not given any food or water. I wondered if we would ever eat again. I had visions of peanut butter and bologna.

Most of all I remember the smell. We were not allowed to go to the bathroom. We had to relieve ourselves wherever we were sitting or standing. People were throwing up, too. The smell of human waste and vomit was putrid. All around us, children were crying, and women were trying to comfort them. My mother's lullabies helped me drift off to sleep, but the heat, the smell, and the noise made it hard to sleep for long.

Every once in a while I heard an eruption of yelling and screaming, then the noise would die down. It was not until much later that I learned the cause of the commotion. Not everyone survived the train ride. Some women and children died from the heat or lack of water, or maybe the anxiety was too much for them. When the guards found them, they would just toss the bodies off the train as though they were sacks of garbage.

When the train finally came to a stop, we were at a place called Gedangan. The soldiers dumped everyone's belongings onto the platform, and hundreds of women and children had to sort through the piles until we found what was ours. There were exclamations of dismay all around us when it became clear that much of what we had packed had not made it onto the train. My mother and Oma were shocked to find all their pots and pans were gone. How were they going to prepare our meals?

From the train station we were taken to a large, empty building that had once been a convent—a home for nuns—and a school. It was built of concrete and tile and had hundreds of dormitory-style rooms. Each person was given a number and assigned to a room. They kept families together, so my mother, Oma, and I were in the same room. Our room was long and narrow, like a hallway, and held about 30 people. There was no furniture except for a strange kind of bed—a long platform with wooden legs to keep it off the cement floor and a thin straw mat for each person to sleep on. There was nothing to separate one person from another or to tell where one person's space ended and the next one's began. There were wooden shelves against the wall for our clothes, soap, and whatever other toiletries we had managed to bring with us.

Our roommates were all Dutch women and children from Surabaya, but none of them were our relatives and none had been our friends or neighbors. They were all strangers. There was a little girl about my age, but we were both very shy. With all the rules in the camp there was no opportunity for us to play together. There were no toys to share—not even a ball, book, or any crayons to color with. She stayed close to her mother, and I was either with Oma or my mother.

We all chose sleeping places on the platform. The person at the end of the platform had the prize position because she didn't have to crawl over a lot of other people to get out of bed. Those places went to women too old to easily maneuver over others. I was proud that my Oma was considered strong even if it meant we had to sleep in the middle. Using chalk from Oma's sewing basket, my mother wrote our names and our assigned numbers in each space so that the others would know that the spots belonged to us rather than to the Schippers or the van Voorts. After a while, of course, everyone knew her place.

For bedcovers we used a thin sheet or whatever piece of cloth we had brought with us. I had a little pillow that my grandmother made for me out of material she had packed. It was tan canvas and had my initials embroidered with red thread. I cherished that pillow. No matter where we went or what happened to us, I could always sleep so long as I had my pillow and Greta.

Our dormitory had small, square windows high on the walls like portholes on a ship. A *klamboo,* a kind of mosquito net, hung from the ceiling. At night, it covered the sleeping platform like a tent. We needed the net because there were no screens on the windows, and nights in the East Indies are full of mosquitoes. It was bad enough that they bit us and left itchy welts, but, far worse, they carried malaria, a disease that causes high fevers and violent shakes—even death. During the day, we tied the klamboo to the side so we could move around.

Everything in the camp was regulated and scheduled. We had to get up at a certain time and go to bed at a certain time. Everyone who wasn't considered too young or too old—in other words anyone between about 11 and 60—had a job to do. Each woman worked for two or three days at a time at one job, then would be assigned to another one—things like sweeping floors, picking up trash around the camp, cleaning toilets, and cooking meals. They also had to clean the soldiers' houses.

In her spare time, each woman was expected to do laundry for herself and any family members. There were no washers or dryers or hot water, for that matter. Even clean water was hard to come by. Often people would share a laundry tub without changing the water. All our clothes and linens were scrubbed by hand, wrung out, and hung to dry on clotheslines strung around our room. In the early days some women who had brought irons with them would press their clothes, trying to keep up a neat appearance. The irons were heated with hot coals from the wood stoves in the camp kitchen. Pulling back the handle on top of the iron opened a metal box, which held the hot coals. There were little holes on the sides of the iron to let out the steam. It was very heavy, like a huge cooking skillet.

Most of the women had always had servants to do their cleaning, cooking, and laundry. But they knew if they wanted food to eat, clean clothes to wear, and a neat place to live, they had to do the work themselves. No one else was going to do it for them. Besides, no one was interested in being reprimanded by the guards.

In the beginning we had enough to eat. There was always rice because that's what the Japanese were used to eating and it was available from plantations on the island. And we had good bread and butter. Some of the women, including my mother and grandmother, used what little money they had been able to keep to buy fresh fish, fruit, and vegetables from an open-air market at the camp entrance. Others traded trinkets or any

clothing they could spare for food. There were
no sodas or fruit juices to drink, but we had water.

The food was cooked in huge iron pots over
wood-burning stoves, much like the one Kokkie
used at our home in Surabaya. When it was time
to eat, we stood in line and got our food in the
kitchen on metal plates. Then we would go outside
and sit at assigned places on a ledge that went all
the way around the outside of the building. The
ledge was made out of tile and cement just like
the building itself. I remember that when I sat
on the ledge, my legs would dangle down. The
tile was nice and cool. We sat just like the local
people, making sure to spread our legs so that the
sweaty skin of our thighs didn't stick together.

As our money ran out and the war caused
supplies to become more scarce, we had fewer
and fewer extras. First there was no butter
for the bread, then there were no fresh fruits
and vegetables, and then there was no bread.

There was only rice. I had always thought rice was boring food, but suddenly, when there was nothing else to eat, it became a delicious treat.

There were guards around all the time. Even while we were sleeping, guards would walk in and out of our dormitory. They were constantly giving orders, commanding us to do things that we couldn't understand because they didn't speak Dutch and we didn't speak Japanese. We knew only a few simple Japanese words and expressions like "sir," "good morning," and "thank you."

The soldiers did a lot of arm waving and yelling what sounded to me like *yong, yong, yong, yung, yong*. When we couldn't understand what they wanted us to do, the guards became angry. Their facial expressions would change, and they would start hitting and shoving people around. Even though no guard ever hurt me, I lived in constant fear that one would.

I used to stand and watch the guards, trying
to figure out what they were saying, thinking
what a weird language Japanese was and
wondering why they couldn't talk the way we
did. I thought they were just trying to be mean,
talking that way. It never occurred to me that
Dutch must have sounded just as odd to them.
We children never dared to ask questions.
Everything was always *shush-shush*. Be quiet.
Don't say anything. Just do what you're told.
I always looked to my mother and grandmother
for protection, but even at four, I knew there
wasn't much they could do.

Another job the women had was looking after
children who were too young to be put to work.
They played games like duck, duck, goose with
us preschoolers. They also took turns telling
stories and teaching us nursery rhymes. Some of
these were favorite bedtime stories my mother

told me before the war, but others were brand-new. We used our fingers to draw pictures and hopscotch squares in the dirt.

We were all required to learn how to count in Japanese and how to sing the Japanese national anthem. Some of our teachers were other Dutch prisoners who could speak a little Japanese, some were young Japanese soldiers, and some were interpreters who worked for the Japanese. They would choose a few of us at a time and take us away from our group to work with us. It made me nervous to be in a "class" that had adults as well as teenagers and other kids. I was always afraid that I would be punished for making mistakes. I never was, but the fear was always there.

Counting was important because when we had inspections, we had to say the number we had been assigned in Japanese. Inspections were held outside at least once or twice every day, but not always at the same time. It was like the air-raid siren—always a jarring surprise no matter how often it happened. Because my mother had been chosen as the leader for our dormitory, she was responsible for making sure we lined up in the proper order.

We were inspected by rows. The 50 people in our group (our room and one next to it) would line up in 5 rows with 10 people in each row. We had to line up by our assigned number, from 1 to 10 in the first row, 11 to 20 in the second row, and so on. Each person had to call out her number in numerical order, starting with the first person in the first row. It was essential that we remembered whom to stand next to because things could get confusing very fast. In the hurry of trying to get in line, it was easy to wind up in the wrong place. If this happened, you might say the wrong number. I was lucky because my grandmother was always next to me, and she would whisper my number to me. A person who didn't say the correct number would get pulled out of line, and both she and my mother, as group leader, would be punished. Fear that I might have to watch guards beat my mother made every inspection very stressful for me. I have a vivid memory of her being pulled out of line and slapped on her shoulders and back. The guards yelled something in Japanese, then they took her away—all for someone else's mistake. We didn't see her until bedtime.

After everyone was in her correct place and had called out her number, the inspection would begin. First, we had to sing the Japanese national anthem. This was part of an indoctrination process to make us loyal to Japan. The guards watched and listened to make sure everyone was singing correctly. If a guard thought a woman didn't know the words, he would pull her out of line and make her sing the song alone. If she couldn't, he hit her and the group leader with the flat side of his sword or with a leather strap that some of them carried. If a child couldn't sing the song, the guard would hit the leader and the child's mother. They never punished any of us children, but watching them punish mothers—and my mother, if it involved children in her group— for their children's mistakes always made me feel like throwing up.

My mother says that the commandant at Gedangan was an alcoholic. After a drinking binge, he would order inspections, usually in the middle of the night. Just think what it is like when you are awakened out of a sound sleep at 2 in the morning. You can hardly think. We had to grab our clothes and run. In the rush, it was easy to make mistakes and end up in the wrong place in line. That was, of course, exactly what the commandant wanted. Then he could watch the women being punished. We never knew what was going to happen, so we always lived in fear. The Japanese used this fear to control us.

We had to bow low when we called out our numbers. Bowing is a Japanese tradition. Everyone in Japan bows to people of a higher status. So in our camp, the guards bowed to the commandant, the guards of lower rank bowed to the guards of higher rank and to the commandant, and we prisoners bowed to everyone. As we bowed, we had to greet our captors by saying "Good morning" or "Good day" or "Good evening" in Japanese. No one bowed to us because we were the lowest of the low. They just nodded their heads to acknowledge our bow and greeting. Sometimes they didn't even do that. It was another way they made us feel less than human.

Only children five and under and women over 60 were allowed to take naps. Everyone else was expected to be doing something productive around the camp. One day a woman named Annie was caught taking a nap. While she was sleeping, a Japanese officer on patrol happened to see her. My mother, who was cleaning up the room, tried to warn Annie by quietly calling her name, but Annie didn't hear her. The officer rushed into the room, took out his sword, and poked Annie with it two or three times. She woke up with a start, confused and still half-asleep. The officer motioned for Annie to go outside, but when she tried to get up she fainted and fell to the floor. I can still hear the *thud* she made.

Maybe she passed out from fright, or maybe she was sick or weak from not getting enough to eat. Whatever was wrong didn't matter to the officer. He slashed the clothesline with his sword, tore the clothes off it, and looped the strands of rope together to make a whip. Then he made Annie get up and dragged her outside,

shortly after they were married.

...rd from the right) with ...eighborhood friends.

where he gave her a severe beating. There was nothing anyone could do. Any attempt to help or interfere would have just resulted in more punishments. I could hear her crying and screaming as I sat inside the room, clutching Greta. I was scared to death my mother might be next. But for once, she wasn't punished for the actions of someone in her group.

Annie was never the same after that. She managed to do her work, but she moved like a zombie. One day she was taken out of our dorm room. When I asked my mother where Annie went, she just said, "She's not alive anymore."

There was no privacy of any kind at Gedangan. We couldn't dress and undress or take a bath in private. Our bathtub was a huge watering trough, the kind animals drink from. When we took a bath, it wasn't just one person at a time, it was a large group of women and children, with guards all around. Everyone bathed in the same water, which became dirtier and dirtier. When everyone in the group had washed, the women emptied the trough and cleaned it with brushes and mops. For toilets we used outhouses with half doors so the Japanese guards could keep an eye on us the whole time.

We were constantly being watched. That kind of treatment day in and day out can destroy your spirit. If we thought about our miserable lives too much, we would break down and cry. I kept thinking that I was dreaming and that, like in a fairy tale, a prince would kiss me and wake me up. I daydreamed about my cats and about our vacation home and the silly monkeys at the waterfall nearby. Imagining better times helped calm my soul. Even now, after all these years, I daydream about beautiful lakes, snow-covered mountains, and blue skies whenever I am troubled.

Halmaheira

AFTER ABOUT SIX MONTHS AT GEDANGAN, the commandant announced that we would be going to another camp, but we were not told where it was or how long we would be there. That was the kind of mind game they loved to play with us. We had only a day or two to get things together. Packing our things didn't take long because by this time we had even less than when we started. No one had more than a straw mat and a small satchel of clothes. All I owned were two dresses, two pairs of underpants, one pair of shoes, my pillow, and Greta.

On the appointed day we gathered up our belongings and went to the camp entrance, where army trucks were waiting to transport women over the age of 65 and children 10 and younger. This meant that my grandmother could ride with me. My mother had to walk. I felt a certain panic as the scene of saying good-bye to Jack in Surabaya flashed across my mind. I couldn't help wondering if I would ever see my mother again. What if something happened to her along the way or what if she was really being taken to a different camp? My mother seemed to sense my fears. When she kissed me goodbye, she promised me that we would be together again soon. I had to believe she was right.

There were not enough seats for everyone in the back of the truck, and Oma hesitated before taking one. A guard ordered her to sit down, but she didn't understand what he was telling her. When she didn't move fast enough, he jabbed her with the bayonet on the end of his rifle. She sat down after that. But the bayonet had broken the skin, and her wound became infected. Without proper treatment, it took a long time to heal.

Halmaheira, our new camp, was in Semarang, the town where my grandfather had once been city administrator. I am sure he never dreamed the Japanese would one day hold his wife, daughter, and granddaughter prisoner within its limits. Halmaheira was a much bigger camp than Gedangan, housing almost 4,000 women divided among several compounds. We lived in bamboo huts instead of cement dormitories. There were eight women in our hut, counting my mother, my grandmother, and me. I was the only child.

The hut had a thatched roof and torn and tattered screens, which offered little protection from flying insects. There was a doorway but no door. That was it. There was no furniture. Everybody slept on the ground on straw mats. There was no place to cook anything because all of that was done in a camp kitchen. There was no electricity, but that didn't matter much because daylight lasts a long time in the tropics. The leaders were given flashlights in case they had to get around after dark. My mother used hers for going to work in the kitchen before the sun came up.

Just as at Gedangan, the women all had chores to do. My mother's primary job was working in the camp kitchen. She worked there every day of the nearly three years we were imprisoned at Halmaheira. I hardly saw her at all during this time. Kitchen work required very long hours because there were so many people to feed and not enough cooking utensils to cook for everyone at one time. We ate in shifts. And then, of course, there was the cleanup.

The stoves burned wood for fuel. Each day my mother had to go with a group of other women into the forest outside the camp and cut down small trees with a machete. The daily hacking and hauling took their toll on her hands, elbows, arms, and back. She still suffers from the recurring pain.

The food at Halmaheira was mostly rice and not enough of that. We ate very little protein, so the women were always on the lookout for wild animals they could catch. Every so often strays would show up in camp. We saw dogs, an occasional cat, monkeys, and turtles. Sometimes they ended up in the cooking pot. There were snails and slugs all over the place, especially during monsoon season. We kids would get empty food cans from the camp kitchen and go out hunting. We would walk slowly around the camp, our eyes peeled for the little beasties. It became almost a game to see who could fill their can the fastest. I never did like touching slugs—they were too slimy. But snails are neat and tidy in their little shells. I had no problem picking them up. It made us feel good that we were helping to put food on the table. At the end of the day we could look forward to eating boiled snails with our rice. They were delicious.

On rare occasions we had fish. More often than not the vegetable was cooked grass. We also ate the bananas and coconuts that grew in abundance all around the camp. And we ate a lot of laundry starch. The women discovered that if they cooked the starch and allowed it to cool, it would thicken like jello. It doesn't taste like much, but we ate it mixed with ground sambal to spice it up. Sambal is a small, hot pepper eaten throughout the East Indies. When it turns from green to red, it's ready to pluck. There was a lot of it growing around the camp.

The first Europeans who came to the East Indies more than 300 years before I was born became rich from trading in the spices that grow on the islands. And here we were—the descendents of those Europeans—using those very same spices to make our imprisonment slightly less unpleasant. When it was time to eat, we would go to the camp kitchen and stand in line holding empty tin cans—the same ones we used to collect the snails and slugs. As we moved along, food was spooned into each can. We ate outside, sitting on the ground.

Fights sometimes broke out during mealtime. Arguments erupted when some people tried to take more than their share. Terrible as the food was, it was better than going hungry. One of my mother's jobs was to act as sort of a food cop and restore order before the guards came. Their solution would be to just take the food away. No one was interested in missing a meal.

To help me forget how hungry I was, I would think about what I used to eat at home. I imagined having a whole jar of sticky peanut butter. I conjured up the smell of bologna sandwiches and the aroma of Kokkie's kitchen. I re-created in my mind the salty taste and crunch of the egg rolls we bought from the Chinese food vendor. I loved egg rolls. I still love egg rolls.

One of my mother's tasks was to make sure the buckets that served as toilets were emptied on a regular basis. There was even less privacy for using the toilet at Halmaheira than there had been at Gedangan. There were no outhouses with half doors. All the toilets were buckets out in the open on raised platforms. There was a rim around the edge of the platform, which was supposed to keep any overflow from running onto the ground. You had to sit on the bucket to go to the bathroom. If you wanted any sort of privacy, you had to find someone to hold a sheet or piece of cloth around you. Eventually we learned to wrap ourselves when we sat on the toilet so the guards couldn't see. It was a small but important victory in our battle to preserve a little dignity.

There was no toilet paper. Instead, each toilet area had a water hose and a soap dish so we could wash ourselves. For washcloths we used rags from worn-out clothing. We also used rags to blow our noses. We had to use those same rags over and over again. If you were lucky enough to get a clean rag, you used only a little corner to blow your nose, and then you rolled it up. The next time you had to blow your nose, you used another corner.

When a waste bucket was full, it would have to be removed and emptied. This was a constant chore because it didn't take long to fill the slop buckets when so many people with diarrhea were using them. At first, it only took two women to carry one of the large, heavy buckets. Each bucket had a handle on it. The women would put a thick bamboo pole through the handle and then, with one woman at each end of the pole, they would lift the bucket and hang the pole across their shoulders. They carried the bucket to a ditch at the other side of the camp. It was a good 15- to 20-minute walk in the hot sun. Over the years, the women grew weaker from lack of nourishment, so it took the efforts of four and sometimes even six women to lift and carry the full waste buckets.

When my mother carried her end of the pole, she bounced a little bit as she walked. She told me this made it easier to carry the heavy load. The trick was not to bounce too much because that would cause the waste to slop out, and there would be a yucky mess to clean up.

Once my mother was punished because the guards said the buckets she was responsible for had not been emptied on time. One of them yanked her so she fell and hit her back on a curb, and then he kicked her. She was hurt and couldn't get up, but nobody dared to lend her a hand. Eventually she managed to stand by herself. I watched the whole thing from our hut, and I wanted so much to help, but I knew if I did the guard would just hurt her more.

Keeping ourselves clean and healthy was a serious challenge. Our mothers tried to get us to take care of our teeth, but we didn't have toothbrushes. We used our fingers or little pieces of wood. I had to brush my teeth with paste made out of ashes. It was vile, and my teeth felt gritty afterwards.

It was almost impossible to keep our hair clean and combed. There were no scissors, so everybody's hair was long and matted. Lice were rampant; everyone had them. Since we slept together, the critters could easily scurry from one head to another, so it was impossible to get rid of them. Washing did help somewhat with the itching, but we had no medicated shampoo—just bars of hard soap.

Clothing was always a problem. Mostly we only had the clothes we had packed when we left home. Everything was either torn, worn out, or too small—from growing up, not out. At age six and seven I was still wearing outfits my mother had bought me when I turned four. Sometimes the Japanese gave a sort of uniform (something like a housecoat) to the group leaders so they would stand out in a crowd, and once in a while the commandant of Halmaheira allowed the Red Cross to bring clothes to the camp. Visits by the Red Cross were something provided for in rules of war called the Geneva Convention, but the Japanese did not feel bound to honor them.

Red Cross days were exciting days. There was never anywhere near enough clothes to go around and rarely was anything a perfect fit, but any "new" piece of clothing was cause for celebration. It is impossible to describe the thrill of seeing the Red Cross trucks arrive. Oma and I would go together because my mother was almost always working. I would stand there, barely able to keep from jumping up and down as she held something up to me for size. (We weren't allowed to try the clothes on so they would stay as clean as possible for the next stop.) I would hold my breath and cross my fingers, toes, and anything else, praying that she would say it fit. If it did, and if she didn't think there was another girl more desperately in need of it than I was, I would get it. I only got one new outfit this way, but it made me feel like a princess.

We girls wanted so much to be pretty. We braided each other's matted, lice-infested hair and decorated our dirty, undernourished faces. We were fascinated by the Japanese women who sometimes visited the guards. They looked so beautiful with their white face powder and very red lipstick. We didn't have makeup, but, thanks to the Red Cross, we did have a white talcum-like powder. We put that on each other's faces so we would be pale like the Japanese ladies. And we rubbed our cheeks with colorful flowers, though we were careful not to touch the flowers to our lips in case they were poisonous.

It is amazing how everyday life continues even under the most extreme circumstances. There were lots of children at Halmaheira, and we escaped the hunger and deprivation in play.

Hide-and-seek and let's pretend were two of our favorite pastimes. During the monsoon season's hard rains, we were allowed to run in the rain and splash in the puddles. This was also when we played "airplane." We would stretch out our hands and arms and run with the rain in our faces and the wind at our backs. The wind helped us run faster and made us feel free.

Sometimes we had paper and pencils from the Red Cross, but such treasures were rare. There was never enough to go around, so we always had to share. We would create designs in the paper by punching little holes in it.

We made most of our toys ourselves. To make a doll of wool yarn (another gift from the Red Cross), we looped the threads together, then tied a button or seed pod on for the head. We strung a bunch of yarn on each side to make arms. Then all we had to do was name her, and she was ready for any adventure we could imagine.

We made whistles out of the big, glossy banana leaves that grew around the camp. We would take a leaf and fold it in half lengthwise, pinch it at the end in a cross pattern, then stick it into our mouths and blow. We delighted in the harsh sound because it drove the adults crazy.

We learned how to do things with our hands. We would weave our fingers together to make patterns like cat's cradle. We put our hands together inside out, then opened them up as we chanted, "Here's the church, here's the steeple, open the door, and see all the people."

The women took turns keeping us busy and giving us a little schooling. They used sticks to teach us addition—1 stick plus 1 stick makes 2 sticks, 2 sticks plus 1 stick makes 3 sticks, up to 10. I learned my multiplication tables by clapping my hands while repeating, "1 times 1 is 1. 2 times 1 is 2." With the clapping, learning math was like learning a song.

There were no children's books, but I learned to read a few simple words that were drawn in the dirt. The older women told us stories. Some were folktales, some they just made up.

Singing was a favorite pastime. We had sing-alongs, especially toward twilight. My mother would lead the singing. Whoever felt like it—adults and children alike—would join in. We had long narrow pieces of wood that we clapped together as we sang. One of my favorite songs was about two children under their mother's umbrella. It made me think of Jack and hope that he was singing too, wherever he was.

We spent nearly three years at Halmaheira. In all that time we got to know the personalities of our guards. They weren't all mean. The younger ones were sometimes more lenient—especially to us kids—than the older ones. We even came to think of one, a watchman whose post was near our hut, as our friend. He didn't get so upset with us if we forgot to bow or how to say something in Japanese exactly right.

The adults, however, always had to be careful. Group inspections at Halmaheira were similar to those at Gedangan. We each had a number, and we had to line up in numerical order. The guards were constantly watching to catch someone doing something wrong. If anyone talked during inspections, the guards would become agitated and start yelling. I suspect it was because they didn't know what the women were saying. But put yourself in the shoes of a prisoner. Imagine how panicked you would be if you were being told to do something in a language you didn't understand, and you knew you would be punished if you didn't follow orders. Most likely you would ask someone around you what was being said. That's what my grandmother would do. My mother was called

"Sis" because she was the youngest one in the family. I remember my grandmother saying to my mother, "Sis, what do you think he's saying?" or "Sis, I don't understand." Usually, but not always, my mother could figure it out. Or maybe she was just good at making lucky guesses.

Whenever anyone was singled out for severe discipline, all of us—even the youngest children—had to watch. We were told the same thing would happen to us if we did what the person being punished did. It was another example of control by fear.

About a year after we arrived at Halmaheira, two women received a terrible punishment for stealing food. They sneaked into the guards' vegetable garden early one morning, about 3 or 4 a.m. Food was getting scarce, and they were desperate for something to eat. There must have been some sort of alarm that only went off in the guardhouse, because they were caught.

Later that day we all had to witness their punishment. The guards built a cage around them with chicken wire. They were tied to a fence with their hands behind their backs, and then cords were strapped across their bodies so that they couldn't bend down. They had to face the sun. No one was allowed to give them any food or water. The women died a slow death, from sunstroke or dehydration or maybe both.

Because of the poor diet and lack of sanitation, Halmaheira was riddled with disease. Soon after we arrived, I came down with malaria, and I suffered from it off and on throughout my time at the camp and long after—until I was 14! I had spells of high fever and uncontrollable shaking that come with malaria. When the fever set in, I would be really sick for a day or two. I was in too much pain to move, and despite the heat, I couldn't get warm enough. I would just lie on my mat in the hut all day. The fever made me delirious, and my skin turned yellow because the disease affected my liver. When I awoke from that initial stage of high fever and terrible sweats, I would be completely exhausted. It took me a couple of days to recover enough so that I could start eating and going outside again.

We didn't have a thermometer, so I never had my temperature taken. My mother just put her hand on my head to feel how hot I was. She or my grandmother put wet rags on my forehead to get the fever down. Mostly it was Oma who held me during the attacks while I cried and cried.

I was lucky to live through my illness. Not everyone did. Two women who lived in our little hut died, one of them from typhoid fever, the other from intestinal worms. I don't know what caused the worms, but they were long and off-white in color. They came up from the woman's belly into her throat and made her choke. To give her some relief, my mother and the other women in the hut pulled the worms out of her mouth. I couldn't watch. It was too disgusting. She would feel better for a few days, then it would start all over again. She was just riddled with worms. All of our diseases—the malaria, the typhoid, and the worms—were curable, but we had no medical care. If we had, perhaps those two women—and so many others—would not have died.

When someone died, her companions had to bring the body to a little compound. The bodies were loaded onto trucks and taken away for disposal. My mother and grandmother tried to shield me from seeing that sort of thing, but once I saw a pile of bodies. I was about five years old, and I did not understand that they were dead. I watched as two guards picked up bodies from the pile. One held the arms, and the other held the legs. Then they tossed the bodies onto a truck.

It reminded me of a game called "walrus" that we had played before the war. My father and mother would take my hands and feet and swing me, singing something like "walrusing, walrusing, da da da,"—I don't remember the exact words—then throw me onto the bed. I thought the Japanese soldiers were playing that little game with the bodies. But then I realized that the people didn't move after they landed. I couldn't understand why they didn't laugh, or cry, or yell, or do anything. I remember one woman in particular. She had short gray hair, and she was tall. When they threw her into the truck, she flopped like a doll.

My grandmother wasn't nearby, so I asked a woman who was watching all this with me what was happening. She tried to explain that the people were not alive, but she didn't want to scare me. She said that those women couldn't walk or talk or breathe anymore, so they were being moved. Not until years later did I realize what I had seen. It makes me shudder to think that this could have been my fate if I hadn't had my mother and my grandmother to look after me. Oma almost always had me by the hand, so I always felt protected and loved.

Every night, starting at Gedangan, my mother and I would say our prayers, simple ones like "now I lay me down to sleep." They were very comforting, and bedtime became my favorite time of the day. It was the one time when I didn't feel so anxious. During the day, I never knew when the siren would sound for inspection, when someone might get yelled at or hit, or if there was going to be enough to eat. This constant state of not knowing what was going to happen has left its mark. I try to hide my fears, but I still have nightmares and wake up in a panic.

We always prayed that we would see my brother and father soon. We looked at the star that my mother had promised my brother we would watch every evening, and she encouraged me to tell the star anything I wanted Jack to know. We talked about home, Kokkie and the others, and about our pets—especially my cats.

My mother told me lulling stories of how we would all be together after the war and what we would do when Pappie returned. "We'll go swimming," she would tell me. "We'll buy pretty clothes and eat egg rolls every day, and go anywhere we want anytime we want." We would be a complete family again. Of course she had no idea if any of this would come true. She didn't even know whether my father or Jack was alive. But she never gave up hope. Her courage gave us the strength to get through the darkest days.

Rumors were running through the camp that

when the war was over, the Japanese were
going to ship all of us to Japan. There, young
girls like me would become geishas, women
trained from childhood to entertain men
with conversation, dancing, and singing. The
older women like my mother would be forced
to become prostitutes. Though I really didn't
understand what any of this meant, the rumors
heightened the anxiety level in the camp. The
amazing thing is how few people broke down.
We couldn't allow ourselves to wonder, "Am I
ever going to be free? Am I ever going to have a
normal life again?" Somehow you force yourself
to believe everything will be OK.

Reunion & Tragedy

◇◇◇◇◇◇◇◇◇◇◇◇◇◇◇◇◇◇◇◇◇◇◇◇◇◇◇◇◇◇◇◇◇◇◇◇◇◇◇

I N HALMAHEIRA, THE ONLY REALITY WAS THE LIFE
of the camp. We knew nothing of what was
happening in the outside world where World
War II raged on. When we went into the camps
in the spring of 1942, Hitler controlled most of
mainland Europe and was fighting the Soviets in
Leningrad (now St. Petersburg, Russia). Victory
over the Soviets would extend his empire to the
borders of Japan's new empire in Asia. So far
as we knew, Japan still dominated the Pacific
region. News of the tide-turning American

victory at the Battle of Midway in early June had not reached us before we entered the camps. By the time the war was over, at least 50 million people would be dead, most of them civilians— some of whom were interned the way we were by various governments. The Germans imprisoned and killed close to 12 million people, most of them Jews. The United States put people of Japanese descent (even if they were U.S. citizens) in camps too, although most of them survived and were released after the fighting was over. In the East Indies people of German descent were interned by the Dutch government in 1940 but released when Germany's ally Japan invaded the islands in 1942.

The war in Europe ended with Germany's surrender on May 7, 1945. Then, in August 1945, the United States dropped two atomic bombs on Japan, killing at least 100,000 people in Hiroshima and Nagasaki. Japan surrendered less than a week later, on August 14, 1945.

Soon after, the miracle we had been praying for happened. Allied planes circled overhead and dropped packages into the camp. I was in bed recovering from a bout with malaria, so at first I didn't see the planes, but I heard their roar. It was the same roar that had come from the planes that bombed our neighborhood in Surabaya. But now instead of hiding, women poured out of every hut. My mother gathered me up in her arms and carried me outside so I could join in the excitement.

Women and children ran around gathering up the bundles and collecting them into a big pile. It was like Christmas. I expected the guards to stop the party and take our packages away, but they didn't. They just watched as we ripped them open and found them filled with food and even goodies like candy. We could hardly believe it. People were screaming and crying, "The war must be over. Maybe this is freedom."

We all stuffed ourselves. I remember jam, peanut butter, and all kinds of unfamiliar foods in cans and jars. Many women, including my mother and grandmother, got sick after eating the rich food. Our bodies had become used to hunger, and our digestive systems couldn't handle so much plenty. Some people who were already very sick died because their bodies were too weak to deal with the diarrhea and vomiting that eating it caused. It would take time for our bodies to readjust to our old diets.

Soon after the first care packages were dropped, the camp commandant summoned the group leaders and told them that the war was indeed over. The Netherlands was once again in control of the Dutch East Indies, even though the Japanese had promised independence for the islands. This would soon create new problems for us, but for now we reveled in our freedom.

We continued to live in the camp until our liberators could figure out a plan for taking care of the sick and getting the rest of us out safely. But the gates were open. We were no longer prisoners. The Japanese guards were still there, but they didn't dole out punishments anymore. We could move around and set our own schedules. We could talk while we ate. There were no more inspections. We could even leave the camp to trade some of our new food to local farmers for fresh fruits and vegetables.

Life in the camp was much more relaxed, but it was as if we were in limbo. We played. Our mothers did chores and kept the camp clean. They were talking about the future, not as if it were a dream but as if it were really about to happen. There was a lot of talk about searching for loved ones, but nobody knew how to begin. For almost four years we hadn't been able to find out who was dead and who was alive.

Within a week or two after the packages were dropped, soldiers parachuted into our camp. They were Gurkhas from Nepal, part of the British forces. They had come to protect us from a new enemy—Indonesian nationalists. Two days after Japan surrendered to the Allies, Sukarno, leader of the revolutionaries, declared that the Dutch East Indies no longer existed. The islands would now be the independent country of Indonesia. (The Dutch government did not officially recognize the independence of Indonesia until December 17, 1949.) The first order of business for the rebels was to get rid of any Dutch people living on the islands.

Once again our world turned upside-down. We and our dreams of life returning to normal were still in danger, but from the Indonesians, not the Japanese; from outside the camp, not inside. While they waited to be shipped home, the Japanese guards stayed in the camp with the Gurkhas. Now, instead of watching us, they helped protect us from the revolutionaries who had surrounded the camp. The rebels were trying to kill us because we were Dutch. They were shooting at the Japanese for betraying their promise of independence. While we hid from whizzing bullets, the guards shot back, trying to pick off the snipers hiding in the trees. Many of them lost their lives.

One of those killed was the guard who had been our friend. He was on his way to warn us of an attack when a sniper's bullet found him. The bullet from the sniper's high-powered rifle was so hot that it set the guard's shirt on fire. Screaming in pain, he ran into our hut. My mother and the other women bound up his wounds, but they couldn't save him. He died later that night. His death hit me particularly hard. The war was over, but the killing was still going on. It all seemed so senseless. Not even Oma's arms could comfort me that night.

It was easy for the snipers to hide in the forest because the palm trees were huge—much bigger than the ones that grow in Florida. The Indonesians often went barefoot, so their feet were tough and callused. At night they would climb those rough-barked trees and hide with their rifles and ammunition belts behind bunches of coconuts.

Even though the camp was under attack, the British began the work of reuniting the former prisoners from camps all around Java. Each day they would hand out sheets of paper with the names of the men who were coming to Halmaheira to find loved ones. One day Jack's name was on the list.

On the day Jack was to arrive, my mother, Oma, and I were at the main gate bright and early. The camp had a bamboo fence around it topped with barbed wire. There were guard stations along the fence. The Japanese had built these so they could catch or shoot any of us who tried to escape. Now, the fence and its guard stations were there to keep our new enemies out.

A truck arrived, and men and boys began to jump off. Shots rang out. The snipers were shooting at them, and the guards were shooting back at the snipers. Everybody from the truck started running, trying to get inside the camp. They couldn't all squeeze through the gate at the same time, so some ran to the fence and tried to climb over the barbed wire. Jack was one of them. As he scrambled over the fence, more shots rang out. Jack lost his grip and fell into the camp. We ran to him, petrified that he had been shot, but he was all right. He had only been scared by the gunfire. Some of the others were not so lucky. They died before they could reach safety. This scene was repeated every time a truck arrived from a men's camp. Once, the rebels captured two Dutch men outside the gate and cut off their heads right in front of us all.

We met every truck that came to the camp because we were looking for cousins and other relatives. Jack told us that at his camp he had found an uncle from my mother's side. His son and about a dozen of our other cousins were also in that camp. The uncle kept watch over all the young boys in the family. We also found out that the mothers of these cousins had been in Halmaheira all along. We had never seen them because they were spread around in the different compounds. The one person we did not learn anything about was my father.

Jack lived with us in our hut for a couple of months. I was so excited to have him back. He was 13 years old now and in surprisingly good health. He told us that boys in his prison camp had been given wooden guns and were being trained to fight for the glory of the Japanese emperor. They had been taught to march in the Japanese style, to sing Japanese military songs, and to obey orders without questioning them. Fortunately, the war ended before they could be shipped off to Japan.

The Red Cross managed to set up a medical office in the camp. The British supplied doctors and medicines as well as food and clothing. For days the lines to see the doctor stretched all the way across the compound. None of us had seen a doctor in more than three years.

I was the only one in my family who needed immediate medical attention. You see, unless malaria is treated properly, the attacks keep getting worse and more frequent until the patient dies. The doctors didn't think I was going to live, which is why I was one of the first patients to leave the camp. I was taken to a hospital in Bandung, a city about two hours away. There, my malaria was officially diagnosed through blood tests.

While in the hospital, I was treated with several different medications, but the basic treatment for malaria at that time was quinine. It took a while for the drug to be effective, but slowly it began to work. The attacks came further and further apart and were not as intense. I was getting well, but it would take years for the attacks to stop.

The most amazing thing about the hospital was how much there was to eat, the clean sheets, and the comfy pajamas. They were lightweight flannel with alternating wide and narrow white, blue, and rose stripes. They were so soft. I loved them. After about a month, I was moved to a hospital in Batavia (now called Jakarta). My mother, Oma, and Jack moved there, too.

In Batavia, my family lived with hundreds of

other displaced people in a large school building near the hospital. There, everyone slept on mats on the floor. There were lots of rooms, so people weren't all crowded together. My mother used to visit me every day. She would arrive between mid-morning and lunchtime and stay with me until about 7 or 8 o'clock at night. On days when my malaria flared up, she stayed later.

The revolution was being fought on the streets of Batavia, so the Dutch government had set a curfew—a time at night when everyone was required to be home. When my mother stayed late at the hospital, she risked being arrested for violating the curfew as she headed back to the school. And of course she also risked being caught in the cross fire. The fighting usually started around twilight. I could hear the now-familiar sound of whistling bullets from my hospital bedroom.

My mother had always been a risk taker. She

would sneak back to her building by crawling through cement water pipes. She was caught once. Lucky for her, it was by Dutch soldiers. They just gave her a warning and let her go. If the soldiers had been revolutionaries, they would have shot her—or worse.

Rescue

I WAS STILL RECUPERATING IN THE HOSPITAL, BUT I was wearing regular clothes—all gifts from the Red Cross—and could move around a bit. Shortly after lunch one day my mother came in and said, "I have someone here who would really like to see you, but I can't tell you who it is. It's a big surprise." Her face was flushed and she was obviously enjoying her secret.

I couldn't imagine who could be coming. I thought maybe it was my grandmother or Jack.

I kept asking, "Who is it? Who is it?" but she wouldn't even give me a clue.

"No, no," she said, "I'm not going to tell you. Let's comb your hair and make you look pretty." She brushed my hair, which now was free of lice and reached down to the middle of my back, and then tied a big, gold ribbon in it. As she fixed me up, she kept saying, "I can't wait for you to see this person." When she finished fussing over me, she took me by the hand and said, as if signaling someone, "It's all right now."

That's when my father walked into the room. I screamed, "Pappie," and ran to him. He picked me up and hugged me so hard. I hugged him right back. He was just as I remembered him—tall, handsome, and strong. The three of us just hugged, and laughed, and stared at each other as if we couldn't believe we were really together after all this time.

Just as we had no idea about what had happened

to my father, he had no idea what had happened to us. He feared we had all been killed when the Japanese bombed Java. After his plane was shot down and he was rescued, he had been sent to the United States by the Dutch military. Because at the time the Netherlands was in the hands of Nazi Germany, the Dutch government established training camps for their military personnel in countries where no fighting was going on.

After the war, he went to the Red Cross to ask for help in finding his family. My mother did the same thing. He said he was looking for his wife. She said she was looking for her husband. The Red Cross received millions of such inquiries from across the world. This was before computers and the Internet, so combing through all the case histories took a great deal of time.

My mother had learned that my father was alive and in Batavia only a few hours before she brought him to my room. Now that he had returned to us, and despite the revolution raging just outside my hospital window, I believed that everything would go back to normal—just like my mother had promised.

For a short time it looked as if all was well. My father was given a post as a colonel in the Dutch Marine Corps and was stationed in Surabaya. That meant we could move back to our hometown. The move was an adventure in itself. My father flew the military transport that took us home.

We couldn't move into our old house because the revolutionaries had given it to another family, but we lived near enough to it that we could play with the few old friends who had made it back to the neighborhood. Our new house had a piano, and my mother began to play again. My father bought trunks full of cloth and sewing materials, and I got to have lots of clothes made for me. And best of all, my father came home every night for dinner, just like before the war. It was all so wonderful that it was hard to get used to. My first toy in my new home was a ball. A real ball! I was so excited to receive a little ball after almost four years of having nothing store-bought.

The Dutch government reopened the schools even though there was no money to pay teachers and there were no supplies. Only the teachers had books. The school Jack and I were assigned to hadn't been bombed directly, but it had been close enough to the bombing that the pressure had broken all of its windows. The doors were broken too, and the monsoon rains had doused the classrooms for so long that there was mold everywhere. The plumbing was broken, so if we had to go to the bathroom, we tried to wait until we went home for our lunch. If we had an emergency, we went outside (always with a teacher to stand guard in case revolutionaries appeared), dug a little trench in the dirt, used it as a toilet, then covered it up and went back to class. The school needed a lot of work, but it was a place where we could start learning again, and that's all we cared about.

All the schools had been closed for almost four years, so everyone had a lot of catching up to do. It wasn't so hard for me because I was only in pre-school when the war started. But Jack had completed several years of school. Now, at 13, he found himself in the same grade he had been in when he was 10. We learned to write and do arithmetic on the chalkboard because we had no paper, and we each shared our teacher's book when it was time to read. I had learned some math at Halmaheira, but reading was something new and exciting for me.

Sometimes it was hard to concentrate on our studies because the area was full of monkeys. Since there were no windows or doors to keep them out, the monkeys were constantly traipsing in and out of the classrooms. They were quite comical to watch as they checked out all the nooks and crannies, looking for goodies. Usually they took off empty-handed.

After several months, we were moved into a completely renovated school nearby, and I was placed in the second grade. Finally, there were books and school supplies. It was so much fun to sharpen my own pencils. But I had a lot of catching up to do since I had never been in first grade. Basically I had to complete two school years in one.

All this time, while Jack and I went to school and my father went to work on the base, and my mother and Oma worked at getting our house set up again, the revolution was intensifying. It wasn't so bad during the day, but every night as it got dark, new fighting would break out. From our living room, we could hear bullets in the banana trees behind our house. During our lunch breaks and on weekends, we were no longer allowed to play outside. The chance of getting shot was too great. Jack and I made up indoor games to take the place of outdoor activities. We also had lots more time to study our lessons. I spent a lot of time reading with Oma, and sometimes Jack helped me with math. He was always very good at that. I don't think either of us was as nervous about what was going on with the revolutionaries as the grown-ups around us were. We were just glad to be back in a house of our own where the whole family could be together.

Then, abruptly, our window of normalcy closed. One afternoon a soldier friend of my father's came to the door with shocking news. Pappie had been on his way to inspect war damage at a local post office when the jeep he was riding in hit a rebel land mine. He was seriously injured. The soldier took my mother to the hospital where my father was in surgery. Jack and I stayed home with Oma to wait and pray and worry. My father survived the operation but died later that night with my mother at his side. It was the night before their 15th wedding anniversary.

When my mother came home, she was visibly changed. In all our years in the camps I had never seen her look so pale and gaunt. For a moment my mind flashed back to Annie, the woman who had been beaten for napping at Gedangan. My mother hugged both of us, spoke briefly to Oma, and then went to the room she and my father had shared.

The next morning, she took my brother and me to the hospital to see our father. He was laid out on a stretcher in one of the hospital rooms. His swollen face was black and blue and full of shrapnel wounds. Jack managed to hold back his tears, but the shock of seeing Pappie so disfigured was more than I could bear. My mother rocked me in her arms until I quieted down, then Jack and I whispered our goodbyes to Pappie. No one said a word all the way home. I went right to my room and buried my head in my pillow. Jack went for a bike ride to calm his feelings.

But that bike ride just brought more misery. Our new dog, Tippy, chased after my brother, barking. When Jack turned around to see what was going on, he smashed into a parked truck and was knocked unconscious. For the second time in two days, someone came to our door with bad news. A neighbor took my mother to the hospital, where she learned Jack had a concussion. He stayed in the hospital for several days and was released just before my father's funeral.

This was not the last tragedy my mother had to face. The death of my father and the near death of my brother caused her to lose the baby she and my father had recently learned she was carrying. She became extremely depressed. She would sit at the dinner table with us, but she didn't eat or say much. We were all very worried about her, especially Oma. But then, as she had so many times before, she pulled herself together. It must have been sheer willpower. She must have sensed how much we all needed her.

Soon after my father died, it became clear to everyone that the Indonesians were going to win their revolution. The Dutch government began to make plans to evacuate Dutch citizens to the Netherlands. Because my mother, Jack, and I were dependents of an officer in the Dutch Marine Corps, we were eligible to leave with the first group of refugees. The problem was that there was not room for all of us to go at once. Jack was still recovering from his concussion. My mother knew the summer heat in Surabaya would be hard on him, so she decided he should be the one to go. She made arrangements for him to live with some of my father's relatives in the

Netherlands, and we would join him as soon as we could get space on another military transport.

The day we took Jack to the plane was nothing like when I had said goodbye to him at the train station on Darmo Boulevard what seemed like a lifetime ago. This time there was no doubt that we would soon be together again.

Now it was just Oma, my mother, and me again, like in the camps. I started having nightmares. In some dreams I was watching the Japanese march back and forth, back and forth. In others, I was looking for my mother and Oma, running through our house in a panic, sure they were dead. When I woke, I was drenched in sweat. The nightmares went on for years—in fact, I still have them from time to time.

In about a month it was our turn to go to the Netherlands. I learned from Oma that only my mother and I would be going this time. She would have to wait and come later. Although she was my mother's mother, she did not qualify as one of my father's dependents according to military rules.

Why did there always have to be a catch? As much as I wanted to see Jack and to live where there wasn't so much shooting, I couldn't imagine leaving Oma. It would be like living one of my nightmares. A special bond had been forged between us in the camps, and it remained strong after we were freed. She took care of me when I came home from the hospital. She looked after me when my mother was too depressed to think about anything but losing my father and the baby. Oma played with me and listened to me read. It just wasn't right to go off without her.

I did a lot of crying and begging, but my mother's mind was made up. With Jack waiting for us in the Netherlands and the revolutionaries winning the war, she insisted that we needed to leave. A cousin, whose husband was also in the military, would take good care of Oma. It wouldn't be long before there would be space for them to fly to Holland too. Knowing this made me feel a little better, and I began to get excited about the plane ride.

The one advantage to moving was that it took my mother's mind off all of her recent sorrows. She had a lot to do to get ready for the move. For one thing, we would need some warm clothes to take with us. She went through the trunk of fabric that Pappie had bought for us and called the dressmaker. Oma even knit me a sweater to match one of my new wool skirts.

When the day came for us to leave, Oma didn't go to the airport with us. Instead we said our goodbyes at our cousins' house. I was desperately sad, but I was determined not to cry. Somehow I made it into the car. I guess it was knowing we wouldn't be apart forever that saved me.

And Then

HOW DOES LIFE BEGIN AGAIN? I WAS EIGHT YEARS OLD. I had
lived through two wars and the death of my
father. I had spent half my life in concentration
camps. And I had just left the person I loved most
in the world. But of course there was much more
time ahead of me than behind. I slowly settled
into life in the Netherlands and then, a few years
later, to life on Staten Island, in New York City.
My grandmother came for a visit, but she was
uncomfortable in a world where she couldn't

speak the language. It brought back the horrible memory of not understanding the Japanese that she had developed in the camps. I missed her terribly after she went back to the Netherlands, but finally learned to love her from a distance. We kept in touch through letters. She loved to hear all about how Jack and I were getting along.

My mother got a job in New York. Jack and I went to school and then to college. We made new friends, Americans who knew nothing about the internment camps the Japanese had set up on the other side of the world and who had never even been hungry. And we worked hard to make ourselves stop thinking about the past. We pushed those awful years as far back in our minds as they would go. I earned a nursing degree, and got married. My husband and I raised two wonderful children before he died.

Now I am remarried and a grandmother myself. I miss the East Indies, but I love America.

I look at my children and my grandchildren, and I imagine what it was like for Oma all those long years ago. And for the first time, thanks in large part to the support of a loving husband, family, and friends, I am ready to talk, to tell people about my experience. I want to honor the memories of all those who were imprisoned in those camps. And I want you to know what I learned in those terrible camps during that terrible time—to feel compassion for those who suffer, to care for family and friends, and to recognize the right of people everywhere to live free from fear. Most of all, I want my story to be a lesson in the power of positive thinking. It really can turn your life around.

Time Line of the War and More

1939

Germany invades Poland in September, beginning what will become World War II.

In December the United States, protesting Japan's continued aggression in China, stops the export of technical information about the production of aviation fuel to that country.

1940

The parliament of the Dutch East Indies rejects a petition submitted by the Indonesian majority party for autonomy for the Dutch East Indies.

Germany invades and conquers Denmark, Norway, the Netherlands, Belgium, Luxembourg, and France.

Japanese troops begin to occupy the French colony of Indochina, in Southeast Asia. The U.S. responds by stopping all exports of scrap iron and steel to Japan.

In September German planes begin bombing Great Britain. Germany Italy, and Japan become allies by signing the Tripartite Pact and become known as the Axis Powers.

In October Germany begins its campaign to exterminate the Jews in what will become known as the Holocaust.

1941

In January Japan begins planning a surprise attack on the U.S. Naval Base at Pearl Harbor in the Hawaiian Islands.

The U.S. cuts off all oil exports to Japan after that country pushes farther into Indochina.

German troops invade the Soviet Union and begin the siege of
Leningrad (now St. Petersburg) in September. It will last almost two
and a half years, until January 1944.

Japan attacks Pearl Harbor on December 7 as well as the Philippines,
the U.S. islands of Wake and Guam, the Malay States, and Thailand.

Canada and Britain join the U.S. in declaring war on Japan on
December 8, and World War II in the Pacific officially begins.

Three days later Germany and Italy declare war on the U.S., and Japan
invades Burma (now Myanmar).

1942

Japan captures Manila, the capital of the Philippines, in January.
Victory in the Battle of the Java Sea opens the way for Japan to invade
the Dutch East Indies.

On March 9 Japanese forces take control of Java and soon begin
rounding up Dutch citizens for placement in internment camps.
Annelex, her mother, and grandmother will enter Gedangan before
spring is over.

The U.S. government begins its relocation program, forcing thousands
of Japanese Americans into internment camps.

The American victory over Japan at the Battle of Midway on June 4–5
marks the turning point of the war in the Pacific in favor of the U.S.
and its allies.

Japanese troops invade Alaska's Aleutian Islands.

In July Indonesian nationalist Sukarno accepts Japan's offer to lead a
government that is answerable to the Japanese military.

In August U.S. Marines take Japanese-held Guadalcanal in the
Solomon Islands, beginning an "island hopping" campaign designed to
bring U.S. forces closer to Japan.

British and American troops achieve success against the Germans in North Africa in the fall.

Winter weather forces German troops to retreat from Moscow. Annelex and her family move from Gedangan to Halmaheira.

1943

Allied victories over Japanese troops in New Guinea save Australia from the threat of invasion.

Soviet troops defeat the Germans at Stalingrad (now Volgograd) and begin an offensive that will end in the capture of Berlin in 1945.

U.S. forces retake the Aleutians, ending Japan's occupation.

The U.S., Britain, and the Soviet Union pledge to fight together to defeat Germany.

1944

On D-Day, June 6, Allied troops land on the French beaches of Normandy to begin the liberation of Europe.

U.S. Marines defeat the last of Japan's aircraft carriers at Saipan, in the Mariana Islands.

In July U.S. forces take control of Tinian, an island in the Marianas that will become the launch site for bombing attacks on Tokyo.

Paris, France, is liberated from the Germans in August.

The Allies begin the liberation of the Philippines in October.

The Allies begin their drive into Germany in November.

1945

In January Allied forces defeat the German Army at the Battle of the Bulge, in Belgium.

Soviet leader Stalin meets with leaders of the U.S. and Britain in February at Yalta to pledge his support in the fight against Japan. They also discuss the division of Germany and other postwar issues.

In March American B-29 bombers begin their raids on Tokyo. Much of the city will be burned and more than 250,000 Japanese will die.

In April Adolf Hitler kills himself after Soviet troops enter Berlin, Germany's capital.

The liberation of survivors from German concentration camps begins.

May 7 Germany surrenders.

American B-29 bombers drop an atomic bomb on the Japanese cities of Hiroshima (August 6) and Nagasaki (August 9), killing at least 100,000 people.

On August 14 Japan surrenders, ending World War II. Japan agrees to return the Dutch East Indies to the Netherlands despite its promise of independence to Sukarno and his Indonesian nationalists.

Sukarno declares Indonesia's independence from the Netherlands on August 17.

In September Allied forces land on Java and begin the liberation of Dutch prisoners from Halmaheira and other internment camps.

1947
Annelex and her mother leave Java to join Jack in the Netherlands.

1949
On November 15 Annelex, Jack, and her mother begin their life in America on Staten Island, in New York City.

The government of the Netherlands grants Indonesia its independence on December 17. Sukarno becomes the new nation's president.

Illustration Credits

Cover: portrait, courtesy the author, background Tomasz Pietryszek/iStockphoto.com. Insert: pp. 1, 2, and 4 all courtesy the author; map, p. 3 Carl Mehler, Director of Maps, NG Book Publishing Group, Justin E. Morrill, The M Factory, Inc., Map Research and Production; p. 3 lo Semarang Photo Archives/ www.semarang.nl

Founded in 1888, the National Geographic Society is one of the largest nonprofit scientific and educational organizations in the world. It reaches more than 285 million people worldwide each month through its official journal, NATIONAL GEOGRAPHIC, and its four other magazines; the National Geographic Channel; television documentaries; radio programs; films; books; videos and DVDs; maps; and interactive media. National Geographic has funded more than 8,000 scientific research projects and supports an education program combating geographic illiteracy.

For more information, please call 1-800-NGS LINE (647-5463) or write to the following address:

National Geographic Society
1145 17th Street N.W.
Washington, D.C. 20036-4688 U.S.A.

Visit us online at www.nationalgeographic.com/books